RECONCILIATION & REDEMPTION

by

Saint Nektarios Kefalas

Metropolitan of Pentapolis
and
Wonderworker of Aegina

Nun Christina
Anna Skoubourdis

Published by: Virgin Mary of Australia and Oceania 2022 ©
oceanitissa@gmail.com
www.oceanitissa.com.au
Youtube: Oceanitissa

Portrait of Saint Nektarios of Aegina, 2009
Andreea Ioana Bagiu

https://andreeafineart.weebly.com/

"'Father, the hour has come. Glorify Your Son, that Your Son also may glorify You'"
(John 17:1)

The hour has come! The time has come which has been preordained from the foundation of the world for the reconciliation of God and man! O momentous occasion! O advent of sacred moments! What words can describe your sublime character? Your advent has changed everything! And all of creation is renewed! In you the wall of separation of the enmity has been removed, the screen is sundered, the record of our debts is torn up; in you, we approach God being manifested as His sons! The gate to Paradise which was shut before the ages is opened and those outcast to Earth become heirs of the Kingdom of Heaven. Indeed, this is that great time, which divine love has preordained for the salvation of man foreseen. Yet how awesome is the accomplishment of the reconciliation of those redeemed! The drama that unfolds on Golgotha causes all nature to tremble, and the acts that come to pass even stir up the inanimate creation. Who can bear the arrival of this hour? Our Saviour is put to death, offered as a propitiatory sacrifice to God in order to redeem Adam from the curse and from death, and to show him forth as the precious and beloved image of God. But how does man offer himself at this momentous hour? The hour that grants the fulfilment of his salvation?

Man, whom God saves, offers himself as the sharpest sacrificial knife in the work of salvation, and he provides himself willingly for that work; it is only through the greatest of iniquities that we contributed to the work of salvation. What terrible darkness covered the spiritual eyes of man. A moonless night poured out encompassing all, and all walked about in the pitch black as if under a moonless night. O, how man was corrupted! All nature is altered in fear, and man, darkened in thought and hardened at heart, simply remains unfeeling and impassive. The sun is darkened, the light of the moon is hidden, and the earth is seized with trembling, with its innards torn asunder; the dead sense the events taking place, while the living are shown to have less sense than the dead; the stones are sundered more easily than the hearts of men, the veil of the temple is torn, all things are overwhelmed, and only man, in the general commotion of the world, remains unfeeling and impassive.

And what an antithesis of dispositions there is amongst the persons who are struggling! Divine and human nature contend with one another; the divine, in order to save the human, and the human, in order to destroy itself. How much does God love man; how great is divine love! With what words shall I hymn God's love for man? And what shall I say regarding mankind's hardness of heart and spiritual blindness? How great was Adam's transgression, that man's redemption was accomplished in such a marvellous manner! How great was the cost of our redemption! Truly, this hour is great. Indeed, it is great and sacred and holy! For it is the hour of reconciliation, the hour of redemption.

So then, because the topic of my homily is dictated by the subject matter of the Gospel passage, I shall speak about reconciliation and redemption.

PART ONE

THAT MAN SINNED AGAINST GOD.

As we come to the explanation of our topic, I think it necessary to include the issue of sin and to examine in terms of how sin actually exists as well as its origin, so that through the testimony of the facts we might proceed to our task without error.

Taking into consideration the earthly life of man, we think that man could not have been fashioned by his Creator in the state that many uncivilized people live in to this day, that is, wretched[1] and miserable, as if man were outcast by nature. For this interpretation is rejected by divine justice. For indeed if it has proved so just to all created things in general, so as to abundantly endow both the fauna and the flora with all the necessary resources for existence, perpetuation of their species, and a pleasing life, it could not justifiably neglect man. Yet the wretchedness and misery of man from his appearance on the earth until today is remarkable: wretchedness and misery of all varieties, like a chameleon or a slithering serpent, plague all of the classes of men, from the savage Indian[2] to the noble

---

[1] κακοδαίμων.

[2] Here Saint Nektarios is referring to the people of India.

European, extending their dominion overall. In creation, man alone is an unhappy being and likewise he alone occasionally calls the happiness of the irrational animals blessed. How strange it is for the most perfect of the created beings to be jealous of the happiness of creatures that are by nature lower than he is! And who can argue against these things or deny the superiority of man? The superiority of man is most apparent from its effects. Man, as the anthropological and psychological studies prove, was created to conceive the idea of universal reality and to encompass it. Man alone is capable of thinking abstractly, judging, and contemplating, he alone can encompass the whole of nature, while exempting himself alone as the one who encompasses; for only that which encompasses is unable to be encompassed. Thus, only man can be outside of the world and objectively view it as other than himself, and consequently as dissimilar. Thus, man, as dissimilar to matter, is most certainly spirit, a spiritual being, a rational being, a being exceptional and superior in creation. He is a being destined to subject all things "under his feet"[3] and from his eminent position to decide concerning the existence or non-existence of the cosmos. Thus, man is excellent since he is distinguished by many excellent advantages. Moreover, if love is

[3] Psalm 8:6.

determined by the favours of goodwill, and its greatness is determined by the quality of the favours, it follows that God's love for man is the greatest love, because only He was endowed with so many great advantages, as so many indicators of divine goodwill.

But if this eminence is a favour of divine goodwill, where do the wretchedness and misery of man come from? If we examine the divine properties, we will solve our query. From the study of created things we draw the conclusion that justice is one of the properties of God. This property of goodness, to which all of nature bears witness, brings us to the following dilemma: we must either concede that God is good and just towards all nature and unjust towards man alone, which also contradicts the particular love of God for man that we indicated above, because the properties are mutually exclusive and cancel each other out, or else concede that man is the cause of his own condition. And because, as demonstrated, God cannot have mutually exclusive properties that cancel each other out, it follows that man is the cause of his own condition; from this syllogism it is clear who is responsible, but now we must seek the reason for the responsibility. In the account of the first human beings in paradise, the Holy Scriptures teach us the reason. From it we learn that the sin of man against God is the sole original cause of his condition; this explanation is true insofar as responsibility is attributed to man and insofar as the magnitude of his misfortune corresponds to the greatness of his sin. Thus, truly, the cause of man's wretchedness is sin against God, which alienated him from Divine Grace, derailed him from the path designated by his own Creator, led him astray into lands of hardship and wretchedness, and made him a pitiable fallen creature both worthy of divine compassion and divine mercies.

MAN NEEDED A DIVINE-HUMAN[4] SAVIOUR FOR RECONCILIATION AND REDEMPTION.

Having demonstrated sin to be the cause of the condition of man, we now seek to learn whether man was able to be saved on his own.

The knowledge of the nature of sin and the condition of man leads us to give a negative answer to this question right from the beginning. And so we say that it is not possible, because sin against God, which is enmity and injustice before God, alienated man from God and severed all communion with him. And if salvation were reconciliation with God,

[4] The "God-Man".

who amongst men could take up the work of the Messiah, to draw near to the divine, to give satisfaction and to bring about reconciliation and redemption? Who could take up this great work, which is exalted and holy, since all of humanity was subject to sin? Who could reconcile both sides and return peace between God and man? For sinning against God is war with God, since he who sins is considered an enemy of God. The Intercessor had to be free of sin, because how would it be possible for one who does not drive away sin to come into relationship with the divine, the pure, the holy? Thus, he needed to enter through a new creation, because none of the created beings could represent man. He who sins must give satisfaction, but being unable because of sin he either had to perish or be saved through a new supernatural creation of God. Divine love chose the second; He sent the New Adam from heaven so as to save man. This New Adam from heaven needed to be a God-Man, so that He might have affinity with both God and man; He unites both [i.e. divinity and humanity] in Himself and with each He speaks its native language, that He might complete the work of Redemption. Our Lord Jesus Christ bore these properties, and hence He became the Saviour of the human race and the ruler and perfector of our nature. For He reconciled us with God, He saved us from enslavement to the

Devil, and made us sons of God the Father and heirs of His heavenly kingdom.

PART TWO

THAT THE ADVENT OF THE DIVINE-HUMAN MEDIATOR WAS FORETOLD BY THE PROPHETS OF GOD AND BY THE GENTILES.

God, in His love for mankind, predestined the perfection of mankind in His plan for creation, that is, a miracle at which humanity would arrive at and which would signify the meeting point between Divinity and humanity, when the Divinity would empty itself in order to come into relationship with the world. This plan in the mind of God was first proclaimed directly after the fall of Adam in the form of the work of redemption, which man then had need of, when He spoke these words to the serpent: "And I will put enmity between you and the woman and between your seed and her seed; he shall watch against your head, and you shall watch against his heel."[5] These words were the promise to man proclaiming the good news of the future advent[6] of the Saviour. All the divinely-inspired prophets, illuminated by the Holy Spirit, saw this promise

[5] Genesis 3:15.

[6] The visit of a king or emperor.

fulfilled and predicted it to the Jews. In prophesying the Advent of the Messiah to the Jews, Moses the Great said, "The Lord God shall raise up a Prophet unto us from our brethren who is like me (a new lawgiver and redeemer), harken unto him in whatever he says unto us. And whosoever does not heed this prophet, shall be cast out from the people."[7] Isaiah, the Most Mighty Voice,[8] proclaimed the Saviour as descending from Jesse like the bud of a tree. "And there shall come forth a rod out of the root of Jesse, and a blossom shall come up from his root: and the Spirit of God shall rest upon him, the spirit of wisdom and understanding, the spirit of counsel and strength, the spirit of knowledge and godliness shall fill him; the spirit of the fear of God. He shall not judge according to appearance, nor reprove according to report: but he shall judge the cause of the lowly, and shall reprove the lowly of the earth: and he shall smite the earth with the word of his mouth, and with the breath of his lips shall he destroy the ungodly one. And he shall have his loins girt with righteousness, and his sides clothed with truth."[9]

---

[7] Cf. Deuteronomy 18:15-19.

[8] Lit. the one of the greatest voice.

[9] Isaiah 11:1-5.

And who is ignorant of that great prophecy of this prophet through which the greatest of the wonders was proclaimed, that of the Virgin Birth? "Behold, the virgin shall be with child..."[10]

The prophet Isaiah, prophesying of years still far off, describes the son of the virgin as already having been born. "For unto us a Child is born, Unto us a Son is given; And the government will be upon His shoulder. And His name will be called Wonderful, Counselor, Mighty God, Everlasting Father, Prince of Peace."[11] What is clearer than this prophecy? Indeed, the prophet attributes the name of God to a child who is yet to be born! And how could he ascribe all of the divine properties to Him, if the Holy Spirit did not truly reveal unto him the divinity of the child Jesus? How was possible for a Jewish man, knowing only the law, to reveal such things about Him?

The prophet Micah sees the Ruler of the people before all ages coming out of Bethlehem. Behold what he says: "And you, Bethlehem, house of Ephratha, are few in number to be reckoned among the thousands of Judah; yet out of you shall one come forth to me, to be a ruler of Israel; and his goings forth were from the beginning, even from

[10] Isaiah 7:14.

[11] Isaiah 9:6 NKJV.

eternity."[12] Who could this Ruler be, Who would be born in Bethlehem and from Whom the beginning of existence is found from eternity, which is before all ages? How could he possibly say such things about a simple man, if those things are not about the God-Man?

And Malachi says regarding the coming of the Forerunner, "Behold, I send forth my messenger, and he shall survey the way before me."[13]

And Isaiah also hears the voice of the Forerunner preaching repentance: "The voice of one crying in the wilderness, Prepare the way of the Lord, make straight the paths of our God… And the glory of the Lord shall appear, and all flesh shall see the salvation of God: for the Lord has spoken it."[14]

Isaiah foretells the entrance of the Lord into Jerusalem riding upon the foal of an ass: "Rejoice greatly, O daughter of Sion; proclaim it aloud, O daughter of Jerusalem; behold, the King is coming to you, just, and a Saviour; he is meek and riding on an ass, and a young foal."[15] The same prophet,

---

[12] Micah 5:2.

[13] Malachi 3.1.

[14] Isaiah 40:3, 5.

[15] Zechariah 27:9.

foreseeing the betrayal by Judas, determines the amount of silver which was paid for the betrayal, "And they weighed for my price thirty pieces of silver... And I took the thirty pieces of silver, and cast them into the furnace in the house of the Lord."[16] And the Evangelist Matthew in referring to the same passage and attributing it to Jeremiah says, "'And they took the thirty pieces of silver, the value of Him who was priced, whom they of the children of Israel priced, and gave them for the potter's field, as the Lord directed me.'"[17] Regarding the forsaking of Christ by His disciples, David says: "My friends and my neighbours drew near before me, and stood still; and my nearest of kin stood afar off."[18] The same author in different Psalms narrates the sufferings of the Saviour as if he is seeing them in the present. Moreover, Isaiah even describes the reason for which he suffered them: "He bears our sins, and is pained for us... But he was wounded on account of our sins... and by his bruises we were healed... and the Lord gave him up for our sins. And he, because of his affliction, opens not his mouth: he was led as a sheep to the slaughter, and as a lamb before the shearer is dumb, so he opens not his mouth. In his humiliation his judgment was taken away: who shall

---

[16] Zechariah 11:12-13.

[17] Matthew 27:9-10.

[18] Psalm 38:12.

declare his generation? for his life is taken away from the earth: because of the iniquities of my people he was led to death... for he practised no iniquity, nor craft with his mouth... and he shall bear our sins... and he bore the sins of many, and was delivered because of their iniquities."[19] The same author describes the sufferings of Jesus in the praetorium as if he were an eyewitness: "I gave my back to scourges, and my cheeks to blows; and I turned not away my face from the shame of spitting."[20] He also speaks of how He was numbered among the lawless: "and He was numbered among the transgressors."[21] Regarding those who bore false witness against the Lord, David says: "Unjust witnesses arose, and asked Me of things I knew not," and regarding the Death on the Cross he says: "they pierced My hands and My feet. They counted all My bones."[22] And again he says, "They parted My garments among themselves, and cast lots for My raiment."[23] And who is willing to give us sufficient time to recount all the predictions in which the advent of the Saviour of all,, from His birth until His

[19] Isaiah 53:4-12. Here St Nektarios modifies the original text "He shall bear *their* sins" to "*our*".

[20] Isaiah 50.6.

[21] Isaiah 53:12.

[22] Psalm 22:16-17.

[23] Psalm 22:18.

glorious Resurrection, was foretold in all its details? Certainly, our time is insufficient, and the character of this discourse dissuades us as well.

The coming of the Saviour was such a common expectation that it was also held by the Gentiles. During the last days of the Roman Republic, the Gentiles awaited such a great and special event. The prophecy was brought to Augustus: *Regem populi Romani naturam parturire* [Nature begets the king to the Roman people].[24] Moreover, news had spread all over the East that a man was meant to appear from Judea to be the king of the world,[25] both in *On Vespas* and in Virgil's work *Idyll* XIII[26] (Tacitus, *Hist*. V. 13).[27] According to Soudas and Nikephoros Kallistos, when Augustus came to Delphi and asked the oracle who was going to rule after him, he received the following prophecy as a response:

> The Hebrew youth commands me,
> who am lord over blessed gods,
> to abandon the house and to go back
> to Hades,

---

[24] Suetonius, *Divus Augustus* 94, 3.

[25] Suetonius, *Divus Augustus* 6.

[26] Virgil, *Catalepton VIII.*

[27] Cornelii Taciti, *Historiarum* lib. V, 13.

> 'Depart then, in silence, from our altars.'[28]

A great number of oracles are referenced which bear witness to the anticipation of the Gentiles. This saying of our own Socrates can be considered such an oracle as well: "You will spend the rest of your lives asleep, unless God sends you someone else in his concern for you."[29]

So, all of the nations felt the need for the advent of the Saviour and all anticipated Him, hearkening unto a mystical voice speaking in their hearts. The arrival of the Saviour became all the more desirable, the more that all forms of hope, consolation, serenity, and morality gradually failed, and corruption, irreverence, sorrow, and hopelessness tended to prevail. The coming of the Saviour and Redeemer was absolutely necessary and He had to have absolute authority, that is, divine authority, in order to set firm the already shaken convictions of the people, to inspire religious piety, to fill up the void in their hearts, to satisfy the demands of the spirit,

---

[28] Nikephoros Kallistos Xanthopoulos.

[29] Plato, *Apology* 31a. Retrieved and modified from http://www.sjsu.edu/people/james.lindahl/courses/Phil70A/s3/apology.pdf on 14 March, 2019.

and finally, to renew their civil and ethical life and reform man.

The total corruption of man is written in the pages of his history, and his inability to improve his condition has also been demonstrated. Greece, Rome, and Judea, representing the wisdom of the world in three different forms, were all unable at their own zeniths to manifest the possibility of the perfection of man, and in approaching their decline, they proved powerless to carry out whatever was possible at their height. Human weakness had been manifested, and went ever further into destruction; the gaping void before the feet of man, increasingly broadened by godlessness, threatened the utter devastation of mankind. The situation presented the following dilemma, either a divine visitation for salvation, or utter destruction. Again, divine love wills the former, for man to be saved. The salvation of man is attested to by the existence of the cosmos itself; if it exists, then it exists because man lives; for it is undeniable that the perdition of man would certainly sweep away the existence of the cosmos.

And who can deny this? What man who is good in heart and illumined by the light of Divine Grace does not feel the mystical language speaking in his heart and assuring him about the redeeming power of Christ? Who does not uncover the divine, the holy, the sublime, and the supreme in the accounts about the person of the Lord? What Jew who is not crooked does not uncover the God-Man Christ in these words? Who does not find the supernatural, the wondrous, and the mysterious in His actions? In whom were all the prophecies fulfilled with the greatest fullness? Who, upon studying ancient and modern history and having discovered the salvific effects of Christianity, does not thereafter exclaim with wonder "this is the change of the right hand of the Most High?"[30] Who, upon discovering the calm in the heart of those suffering, the morality in families living in wretched conditions, the endurance in those who are afflicted, and the self-denial of the virtuous, does not marvel at the might of the work of Christ and does not declare Him God from God and Saviour of the World?

Yes, O Christian brothers! Our Lord Jesus Christ is God from God, Light from Light, who descended from Heaven for our salvation, who was incarnate of the Holy Spirit and the Virgin Mary, and became man, and was crucified under Pontius Pilate.

---

[30] Psalm 76:11/77:11, translation accessed from https://www.ellopos.net/elpenor/greek-texts/septuagint/chapter.asp?book=24&page=76 on 25 May, 2019.

So, come, O Christian brothers, let us take up the wings of our intellect and be lifted up a little, and let us direct our course to Golgotha, so that we might behold there the unfolding drama of reconciliation and redemption; let us stand before the Cross of our crucified Lord Jesus Christ and behold His Passion, which He suffers for the sake of our sins; let us fall down before Him on bended knee and declare Him Saviour and Redeemer, let us pledge repentance for our sins and show piety and reverence towards His Blood which is poured out for us, so that we may become worthy of redemption and heirs of the Kingdom of Heaven, of which may we all be made worthy. Amen.

Athens, on the 23rd of March, 1885.[31]

[31] This sermon was most likely actually delivered on 21/22 March, 1885 during the evening Matins Service for Great and Holy Friday.